M000098917

From a
SISTER'S
HEART

Memories and Wishes
from Me to You

RUBY OAKS

Castle Point Books
New York

FROM A SISTER'S HEART. Copyright © 2019 by St. Martin's Press.
All rights reserved. Printed in China.
For information, address St. Martin's Press, 175 Fifth Avenue, New York, N.Y. 10010.

www.stmartins.com
www.castlepointbooks.com

The Castle Point Books trademark is owned by Castle Point Publishing, LLC.
Castle Point books are published and distributed by St. Martin's Press.

ISBN 978-1-250-21429-4 (hardcover)

Cover design by Katie Jennings Campbell
Interior design by Tara Long

Special thanks to Jennifer Calvert

Images used under license from Shutterstock.com

Our books may be purchased in bulk for promotional, educational, or business
use. Please contact your local bookseller or the Macmillan Corporate and
Premium Sales Department at 1-800-221-7945, extension 5442, or by email
at MacmillanSpecialMarkets@macmillan.com.

First Edition: June 2019

10 9 8 7 6 5 4 3 2 1

Contents

INTRODUCTION

There's no one quite like your sister....

She is a shoulder to lean on, a voice of reason, a secret keeper, a source of laughter, and a loving heart. No one will pester you, frustrate you, or challenge you more than your sister, but she will also be the one to encourage you, treasure you, and lift you back up when you are down. Wherever you are, no matter how far, the bond you share with your sister will always hold you together.

Sisterhood is made up of details big and small—from mannerisms you share to clothes you wouldn't, from moments of make-believe and summer vacations, to good days and hard days.

In this journal, you will find a place to record your memories, milestones, and most cherished moments with your sister. Fill out the pages as a fond retrospective or as an ongoing narrative of your sister story.

There may be many parts to your family tree—deep roots that hold firm and sprawling branches—but a sister is the blossom right next to you that makes it all the more special. Share this keepsake journal of memories with your sister and keep track of all of the things that make your relationship unique.

CHILDHOOD MEMORIES

Our First Memories

THE AGE DIFFERENCE BETWEEN US:

me .... / .... you

MY VERY FIRST MEMORY OF YOU:

....

....

HERE IS A PHOTO OF US AS KIDS:

Two Peas in a Pod

WE WERE INSEPARABLE WHEN:

....

....

....

MY FAVORITE CRAFT OR GAME TO PLAY WITH YOU:

....

[*our secret hideout or club:*]

IF WE HAD A SISTER MOTTO, IT WOULD HAVE BEEN:

" ....

....

....

.... "

No Fair!

WE ALWAYS FOUGHT OVER:

....

....

OUR FUNNIEST DISAGREEMENT:

....

....

....

THINGS YOU WOULDN'T SHARE:

....

....

....

THINGS I WOULDN'T SHARE:

....

....

....

YOU ALWAYS GOT AWAY WITH:

....

....

....

I ALWAYS GOT AWAY WITH:

....

....

....

my nickname for you:

I NEVER TOLD YOU THAT I BORROWED YOUR:

....

....

....

Big Dreams

ONE SHARED CHILDHOOD DREAM WE HAD:

....

....

....

OUR FAVORITE MOVIE AND SHOWS:

....

....

....

we knew every word to:

OUR #1 SONG:

....

....

YOUR SISTER SUPERPOWER:

....

....

Little Worries

I DROVE YOU CRAZY WHEN:

....

....

....

YOU DROVE ME CRAZY WHEN:

....

....

....

ONE THING WE COULD NEVER AGREE ON:

....

....

Shhhh...

WE SWORE NEVER TO TELL ANYONE THAT:

....

....

No Competition

YOU WERE TERRIBLE AT:

....

....

I WAS TERRIBLE AT:

....

....

★★★
We always competed for:

....

....

....

WE WORKED WELL TOGETHER WHEN:

....

....

....

You were the best at:

I WAS THE BEST AT:

....

....

....

I ALWAYS ADMIRED YOU FOR:

....

....

....

The favorite child:

Stronger Together

WAYS WE WERE SO ALIKE:

....

....

....

WAYS WE WERE SO DIFFERENT:

....

....

....

WHEN WE WERE TOGETHER, WE WERE USUALLY:

....

....

YOU ALWAYS HELPED ME WITH:

....

....

....

Smart Mouths

WE ALWAYS GOT IN TROUBLE FOR SAYING:

....

....

We couldn't stop quoting:

"

....

....

....

"

YOU STOOD UP FOR ME WHEN:

....

....

YOU ALWAYS TOLD ME TO:

....

....

....

Face Palm!

THE DUMBEST THING WE EVER DID:

....

I EMBARRASSED YOU WHEN:

....

....

YOU EMBARRASSED ME WHEN:

....

....

We thought we were cool when:

WE'LL KEEP THIS AWKWARD STORY BETWEEN US:

....

....

Spiders, Clowns, and Heights—Oh My!

MY BIGGEST FEAR:

....

YOUR BIGGEST FEAR:

....

YOU HELPED ME STAY CALM WHEN:

....

....

YOU SEEMED SO BRAVE WHEN:

....

....

The fears we've conquered:

Favorite Things

YOU WOULDN'T LEAVE THE HOUSE WITHOUT:

....

....

I WOULDN'T LEAVE THE HOUSE WITHOUT:

....

....

The thing we both loved:

YOUR FUNNIEST OBSESSION:

....

....

MY FUNNIEST OBSESSION:

....

....

WE MUST HAVE EATEN OUR WEIGHT IN:

....

....

THE BOOKS WE COULDN'T PUT DOWN:

....

....

HERE'S A PICTURE OF US DOING SOMETHING WE LOVED:

Growing Up

YOU REALLY GREW INTO YOUR:

....

....

....

I finally grew into my:

YOU ALWAYS GOT COMPLIMENTS FOR:

....

....

....

I'M SO GLAD YOU STILL:

....

....

....

20

FAMILY FUN & GAMES

Good Times

WE HAD SO MUCH FUN WHEN:

....

....

....

OUR HAPPIEST HOURS WERE SPENT PLAYING:

....

....

You always wanted me to play:

....

....

I ALWAYS WANTED YOU TO PLAY:

....

....

....

Taking Sides

WE MADE A GOOD TEAM WHEN:

....

....

THE COMPETITION GOT HEATED WHEN:

....

....

Who usually won:

I HATED PLAYING ON A TEAM WITH:

....

....

YOU LOVED TO TEAM UP WITH:

....

....

Children at Play

WHEN WE WERE LITTLE, WE COULD SPEND HOURS PLAYING:

....

....

....

WHEN WE GOT OLDER, WE PREFERRED TO:

....

....

....

THE WHOLE FAMILY WOULD PLAY:

....

....

....

GAME NIGHT USUALLY ENDED WHEN:

....

....

YOU ARE THE REIGNING CHAMPION OF:

....

I HELD MY OWN AT:

....

....

Here's a picture of us having fun:

The Great Outdoors

WE LOVED TO CATCH:

....

....

OUR FAVORITE DAYS WERE SPENT AT:

....

....

When I saw shooting stars, I wished for:

MY FAVORITE MEMORY OF OUR FAMILY
ENJOYING THE OUTDOORS:

....

....

....

TV Time

SHOWS WE LOVED TO WATCH TOGETHER:

....

....

SHOWS ONLY ONE OF US LOVED:

....

....

HOW MUCH TV TIME WE WERE ALLOWED:

....

THE TV CHARACTERS WE HAD A CRUSHES ON:

....

....

THE NIGHT OF TV WE COULDN'T MISS:

....

....

Movie Night

THE FIRST MOVIE WE SAW TOGETHER:

....

....

THE LAST MOVIE WE SAW TOGETHER:

....

....

Our all-time favorite movie:

WE COULDN'T WATCH A MOVIE WITHOUT:

....

....

Sisters are for sharing laughter
and wiping tears.
– UNKNOWN

One Big Happy Family

FAMILY GATHERINGS MEANT PLAYING:

....

....

....

WHEN WE HAD ENOUGH PEOPLE, WE LOVED TO PLAY:

....

....

....

....

[The most competitive
family member:]

THE LEAST COMPETITIVE FAMILY MEMBER:

....

Good Sports

YOU ALWAYS TEASED ME FOR:

....

....

I ALWAYS TEASED YOU FOR:

....

....

YOU GOT SO ANNOYED WHEN I:

....

....

....

I GOT SO ANNOYED WHEN YOU:

....

....

....

I'm sorry about:

I ENVIED YOUR SKILLS AT:

....

....

....

THE GAME I COULD ALWAYS BEAT YOU AT:

....

....

I WISH WE WOULD HAVE PLAYED MORE:

....

....

Dining Out

OUR FAVORITE PLACE TO GO AS A FAMILY:

....

....

....

OUR FAVORITE PLACE TO GO, JUST YOU AND ME:

....

....

....

[*Our favorite dessert to split:*]

THEY KNEW US BY NAME AT:

....

....

....

Ordering In

A BUSY DAY MEANT DINNER FROM:

....

THE BEST TAKEOUT WAS FROM:

....

....

OUR PARENTS NEVER LET US ORDER:

....

....

YOU REFUSED TO EAT:

....

....

Nothing beats your homemade:

The More the Merrier

WE LOVED GETTING TOGETHER WITH:

....

....

....

THE BEST GAME NIGHTS USUALLY INCLUDED:

....

....

SOMETIMES THE ADULTS CHATTED WHILE WE PLAYED:

....

....

....

SOMETIMES THE KIDS CHATTED WHILE THE ADULTS PLAYED:

....

....

....

Grown-Up Gaming

THE GAMES WE STILL PLAY:

....

....

THE TRADITIONS WE'VE KEPT:

....

....

....

THE TRADITIONS WE WERE HAPPY TO LET GO OF:

....

....

....

We should restart the tradition of:

HOLIDAYS, MILESTONES & CELEBRATIONS

Great Achievements

I WAS REALLY PROUD OF MYSELF WHEN:

....

....

I WAS SO PROUD OF YOU WHEN:

....

....

MY BIGGEST TRIUMPH:

....

YOUR GREATEST SUCCESS:

....

Awards we won:

[ ]

Working Hard

MY FIRST JOB WAS:

....

....

YOUR FIRST JOB WAS:

....

....

THE JOB YOU LOVED MOST:

....

....

....

THE JOB I LOVED MOST:

....

....

....

YOU HATED WORKING AT:

....

....

I HATED WORKING AT:

....

....

YOUR DREAM JOB:

....

....

MY DREAM JOB:

....

....

Sisters help make the hard times
easier and the easy times more fun.
– UNKNOWN

First Dates

WHAT I REMEMBER ABOUT MY FIRST DATE:

....

....

What dating was like then:

THE BEST DATING ADVICE YOU EVER GAVE ME:

....

....

....

THE WORST DATING ADVICE YOU EVER GAVE ME:

....

....

....

Great Loves

Our first loves:

[me .... / .... you]

HOW I MET THE LOVE OF MY LIFE:

....

....

HOW YOU MET THE LOVE OF YOUR LIFE:

....

....

MY FIRST THOUGHTS WHEN I MET YOURS:

....

....

WHAT I LOVE ABOUT YOUR RELATIONSHIP:

....

....

Happy Birthday!

MY FAVORITE BIRTHDAY PARTY:

....

....

....

....

THE BEST GIFT YOU EVER GAVE ME WAS:

....

....

....

....

I was so happy to celebrate you turning:

I LOVED WATCHING YOUR FACE
WHEN YOU OPENED:

....

....

....

Something Yummy

It's not a celebration without:

YOUR FAVORITE KIND OF BIRTHDAY CAKE:

....

MY FAVORITE KIND OF BIRTHDAY CAKE:

....

THE RECIPE OUR FAMILY IS KNOWN FOR AT PARTIES:

....

....

....

YOUR GO-TO RECIPE TODAY:

....

....

....

Happy Holidays

Our family's favorite holiday:

....

....

THE PART YOU LIKED THE MOST:

....

....

THE PART I LIKED THE MOST:

....

....

WHO USUALLY CELEBRATED WITH US:

....

....

....

....

THE TRADITION WE MISS:

....

....

....

THE TRADITION WE'VE BOTH KEPT GOING:

....

....

....

HERE'S A PICTURE OF US CELEBRATING:

New Year's Eve

THE BEST NEW YEAR'S EVE I CAN REMEMBER:

....

....

I celebrated with:

OUR FAMILY'S BEST NEW YEAR'S TRADITION:

....

....

....

OUR CRAZIEST NEW YEAR'S RESOLUTIONS:

....

....

....

The 4th of July

MY FAVORITE 4TH OF JULY MEMORY:

....

....

WE ALWAYS WATCHED THE FIREWORKS FROM:

....

....

CELEBRATING THE 4TH OF JULY MEANT EATING:

....

....

....

TODAY, WE STILL:

....

....

Summer Vacation

YOUR FAVORITE WAY TO SPEND THE SUMMER:

....

....

MY FAVORITE WAY TO SPEND THE SUMMER:

....

....

WE COULDN'T WAIT TO:

....

....

HOW SUMMERS HAVE CHANGED:

....

....

[Our favorite summer treat:]

Halloween

MY FAVORITE COSTUME:

....

THE COSTUME OF YOURS I LOVED MOST:

....

THE CANDY WE TRADED EACH OTHER FOR:

....

....

OUR FAVORITE SCARY MOVIE:

....

....

The best thing about having a sister was that I always had a friend.

– CALI RAE TURNER

Thanksgiving

MY FAVORITE THANKSGIVING MEMORY:

....

....

....

WHO WAS USUALLY AT THE TABLE WITH US:

....

....

....

[*The side dish we absolutely had to have:*]

HOW WE CELEBRATE NOW:

....

....

....

A Day Makes a Difference

THE BEST DAY OF MY LIFE:

....

....

....

THE WORST DAY OF MY LIFE:

....

....

....

The day that changed my life:

THE DAY I WAS MOST GRATEFUL FOR YOU:

....

....

SECRETS &
INSIDE JOKES

Make Believe

WHEN WE WERE LITTLE, WE'D PRETEND WE WERE:

....

....

....

WE HAD SO MUCH FUN PRETENDING THAT:

....

....

....

We loved to perform:

OUR FAVORITE PROPS WERE:

....

....

....

Too Funny

WE ALWAYS MADE FUN OF:

....

....

....

WE COULDN'T STOP LAUGHING AT:

....

....

....

[*Our favorite funny movie:*]

NO ONE ELSE GOT THE JOKE WHEN:

....

....

....

THE PERSON WHO MADE US LAUGH THE MOST:

....

....

OUR FUNNIEST FAMILY MEMBER:

....

....

HERE'S A PICTURE OF US CRACKING UP:

My Sounding Board

YOU WERE THE FIRST PERSON I WANTED TO TELL THAT:

....

....

....

YOU WERE THE ONLY ONE WHO KNEW THAT:

....

....

....

I NEVER TOLD ANYONE THAT:

....

....

....

Our silliest secret:

Being Sneaky

WHEN NO ONE WAS LOOKING, WE WOULD:

....

....

....

WE USED TO STEAL BITES OF:

....

....

....

[The one who always peeked:]

THINGS WE DID WHEN WE WERE SUPPOSED TO BE SLEEPING:

....

....

....

Just the Two of Us

OUR FAVORITE THING TO DO TOGETHER THEN:

....

....

OUR FAVORITE THING TO DO TOGETHER NOW:

....

....

WE HAD SO MUCH FUN WHEN:

....

....

IT WAS LIKE WE SHARED A BRAIN WHEN:

....

....

No one understood our:

[ ]

Tattle Tales

YOU RATTED ME OUT FOR:

....

....

....

....

I RATTED YOU OUT FOR:

....

....

....

....

The one, who can't keep a secret.

WE ALWAYS GOT IN TROUBLE FOR:

....

....

....

....

Peer Pressure

YOUR FRIENDS TALKED YOU INTO:

....

....

....

MY FRIENDS TALKED ME INTO:

....

....

....

WE ALWAYS GOT INTO TROUBLE WHEN WE WERE AROUND:

....

....

....

The bad influence in the family was:

Partners in Crime

OUR CLOSEST FRIENDS GROWING UP:

....

....

....

OUR FAVORITE COUSINS:

....

....

....

[What we called ourselves:]

THE FRIENDS WE'VE KEPT:

....

....

....

So Embarrassing!

MY BIG CRUSH:

....

YOUR BIG CRUSH:

....

I CAN'T BELIEVE I USED TO:

....

....

I'M STILL LAUGHING ABOUT THAT TIME YOU:

....

....

I'm still embarrassed by:

Over the Years

HOW OUR SECRETS HAVE CHANGED:

....

....

....

[We could never keep a secret from:]

THE THING WE THOUGHT WAS FUNNY BUT REALLY ISN'T:

....

....

....

THE JOKE THAT'S STILL FUNNY:

....

....

....

Planning Our Futures

WE SHARED A DREAM OF:

....

....

....

....

IF WE WON THE LOTTERY, WE WOULD:

....

....

....

....

YOU ALWAYS WANTED TO MARRY:

....

I WANTED A WEDDING WITH:

....

YOU WANTED TO MOVE TO:

....

I WANTED TO LIVE IN:

....

YOU WANTED TO BE A:

....

....

I WANTED TO BE A:

....

....

I never try to make anyone my
best friend because I already have one
and she is my sister.

– UNKNOWN

My Favorite Secret Keeper

YOU'RE MY FIRST PHONE CALL WHEN:

....

....

I WANT TO BE YOUR FIRST PHONE CALL WHEN:

....

....

I NEVER TOLD YOU THAT:

....

....

....

I always wanted to tell you that:

A SHOULDER TO LEAN ON

Built-In BFFs

I REALIZED YOU'D ALWAYS HAVE MY BACK WHEN:

....

....

I REALIZED I'D ALWAYS HAVE YOUR BACK WHEN:

....

....

I TRUSTED YOU COMPLETELY WHEN IT CAME TO:

....

YOU COULD ALWAYS COME TO ME WHEN:

....

When we became BFFs:

The Big Questions:

WE USED TO STAY UP LATE TALKING ABOUT:

....

....

....

....

Our favorite place to chat:

THESE DAYS, WE TALK A LOT ABOUT:

....

....

....

OUR FAVORITE WAY TO COMMUNICATE:

....

....

The Best of Times

YOU HELPED ME ACHIEVE MY DREAM OF:

....

....

I HELPED YOU ACHIEVE YOUR DREAM OF:

....

....

YOU BELIEVED IN ME WHEN:

....

....

I BELIEVED IN YOU WHEN:

....

....

Always remember that:

[   ]

The Worst of Times

THE HARDEST EXPERIENCE OF MY LIFE:

....

....

HOW YOU HELPED ME THROUGH IT:

....

....

....

A DIFFICULT TIME IN YOUR LIFE:

....

....

I HOPE I HELPED YOU:

....

....

....

First Aid for the Soul

OUR FAVORITE COMFORT FOOD:

....

OUR GO-TO DRINK:

....

OUR BAD-DAY RITUAL:

....

....

....

....

Our standard heartbreak procedure:

Yin and Yang

WE RELY ON EACH OTHER FOR:

....

....

WE WORK EACH OTHER UP ABOUT:

....

....

WE CALM EACH OTHER DOWN ABOUT:

....

....

....

HOW WE BALANCE EACH OTHER OUT:

....

....

....

Cheaper than Therapy

I FEEL SO MUCH BETTER AFTER VENTING TO YOU ABOUT:

....

....

....

I love to listen to you vent about:

I'M GREAT AT STOPPING YOU BEFORE YOU:

....

....

YOU'RE GREAT AT STOPPING ME BEFORE I:

....

....

YOU TURNED BAD DAYS INTO GOOD ONES BY:

....

....

....

You always made me smile when you:

YOU TALKED ME DOWN WHEN:

....

....

....

I TALKED YOU DOWN WHEN:

....

....

....

Lessons Learned

A LESSON WE LEARNED TOGETHER:

....

....

A LESSON WE LEARNED EARLY ON:

....

....

A LESSON WE LEARNED THE HARD WAY:

....

....

A LESSON WE'LL ALWAYS REMEMBER:

....

....

[Your best advice:]

Bullies and Bad Days

YOU WERE THERE FOR ME WHEN:

....

....

....

I WAS THERE FOR YOU WHEN:

....

....

....

HOW YOU STOOD UP FOR ME:

....

....

....

HOW I STOOD UP FOR YOU:

....

....

....

The Little Things

YOU HELPED ME FIGURE OUT HOW TO:

....

....

....

I helped you figure out how to:

YOU WERE ALWAYS BETTER AT:

....

....

I WAS ALWAYS BETTER AT:

....

....

[You're my go-to:]

YOU WERE HAPPY TO HELP ME:

....

....

I WAS HAPPY TO HELP YOU:

....

....

YOU HELPED ME PULL OFF:

....

....

I HELPED YOU PULL OFF:

....

....

The Big Things

YOU WERE THERE WHEN I LEARNED:

....

....

....

I WAS THERE WHEN YOU NEEDED:

....

....

....

THE MOST DIFFICULT CONVERSATION WE HAD:

....

....

THE BEST CONVERSATION WE HAD:

....

....

My Mentor

YOU TAUGHT ME HOW TO:

....

....

I TAUGHT YOU HOW TO:

....

....

Without you, I never could have:

I WAS BY YOUR SIDE WHEN YOU:

....

....

....

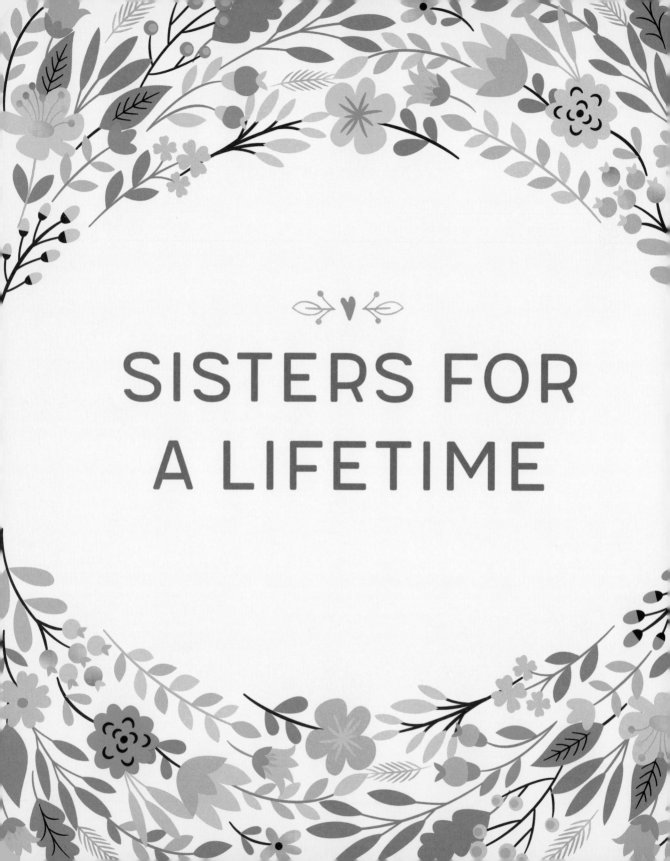

SISTERS FOR
A LIFETIME

My Favorite Memories of Us

AS CHILDREN:

....

....

....

AS TEENAGERS:

....

....

[As young adults:]

IN RECENT YEARS:

....

....

....

....

Keepsakes

THINGS OF OURS I'VE HELD ONTO:

....

....

THINGS I WISH I STILL HAD:

....

....

HERE'S A PICTURE OF YOU WITH ONE OF YOUR FAVORITES:

A TIME CAPSULE OF US WOULD HAVE TO INCLUDE:

....

....

KIDS TODAY DON'T UNDERSTAND:

....

....

....

I WOULD LOVE TO PASS DOWN OUR:

....

....

....

I'M HAPPY TO LEAVE BEHIND THE:

....

....

....

Big Kids

OUR GROWN-UP HIDEOUT OR CLUBHOUSE IS:

....

Now, your sister superpower is:

MY FAVORITE GROWN-UP ACTIVITY WITH YOU:

....

....

YOU STILL WON'T SHARE:

....

....

TODAY, OUR DREAM LOOKS MORE LIKE:

....

....

Unbreakable Bonds

WE'RE BETTER TOGETHER BECAUSE:

....

....

WE COMPLEMENT EACH OTHER'S:

....

....

I'M MOST GRATEFUL FOR OUR MUTUAL:

....

....

The words we live by:

" ....

....

....

.... "

Surprise, Surprise!

LIFE HAS SURPRISED US WITH:

....

....

WE HELP EACH OTHER ROLL WITH THE PUNCHES BY:

....

....

THINGS THAT TURNED OUT BETTER THAN WE EXPECTED:

....

....

....

Things that still might:

Relationship Goals:

THE FICTIONAL SISTERS WE WISH WE COULD BE:

....

....

THINGS WE LOVE ABOUT THEM:

Our theme song:

....

....

....

ONE THING I WANT US TO DO FROM NOW ON:

....

....

....

One thing I want us to stop doing:

The More Things Change

THINGS THAT HAVE CHANGED FOR THE BETTER:

....

....

....

Changes we'd both like to make:

I WILL ALWAYS BE HERE TO:

....

....

....

I'LL PROBABLY NEVER STOP ASKING YOU TO:

....

....

I LOVE THAT YOU STILL:

....

....

I HOPE YOU NEVER STOP:

....

....

HERE'S A RECENT PICTURE OF US TOGETHER:

On My Mind

WHEN YOU'RE NOT AROUND, I MISS:

....

....

....

I ALWAYS THINK OF YOU WHEN I:

....

....

I HOPE YOU THINK OF ME WHEN YOU:

....

....

You're my favorite person
to talk to about:

Hand in Hand

I'M LOOKING FORWARD TO:

....

....

....

TOGETHER, WE'LL TACKLE:

....

....

....

[We'll always make time for:]

EVEN WHEN OUR LIVES ARE CRAZY, WE WILL:

....

....

Our Adventures

MY FAVORITE TRIP WITH YOU:

....

WHAT MADE IT GREAT:

....

....

OUR FAVORITE GETAWAY THESE DAYS:

....

....

OUR TRAVEL BUCKET LIST INCLUDES:

....

....

[Let's plan a trip to:]

Forever and Always

I THINK YOU ARE:

....

....

....

MY LOVE FOR YOU IS:

....

....

....

I want you to remember:

YOU WILL ALWAYS BE MY:

....

....

....

My Hopes for You

IN LIFE:

....

....

....

In love:

....

....

....

IN WORK:

....

....

IN FAMILY:

....

....

....

Get the eBooks FREE!

(PDF, ePub, Kindle, and liveBook all included)

We believe that once you buy a book from us, you should be able to read it in any format we have available. To get electronic versions of this book at no additional cost to you, purchase and then register this book at the Manning website.

Go to https://www.manning.com/freebook and follow the instructions to complete your pBook registration.

That's it!
Thanks from Manning!

Isomorphic Web Applications

UNIVERSAL DEVELOPMENT WITH REACT

ELYSE KOLKER GORDON

MANNING
SHELTER ISLAND

For online information and ordering of this and other Manning books, please visit
www.manning.com. The publisher offers discounts on this book when ordered in quantity.
For more information, please contact

Special Sales Department
Manning Publications Co.
20 Baldwin Road
PO Box 761
Shelter Island, NY 11964
Email: orders@manning.com

©2018 by Manning Publications Co. All rights reserved.

No part of this publication may be reproduced, stored in a retrieval system, or transmitted, in
any form or by means electronic, mechanical, photocopying, or otherwise, without prior written
permission of the publisher.

Many of the designations used by manufacturers and sellers to distinguish their products are
claimed as trademarks. Where those designations appear in the book, and Manning
Publications was aware of a trademark claim, the designations have been printed in initial caps
or all caps.

♾ Recognizing the importance of preserving what has been written, it is Manning's policy to have
the books we publish printed on acid-free paper, and we exert our best efforts to that end.
Recognizing also our responsibility to conserve the resources of our planet, Manning books
are printed on paper that is at least 15 percent recycled and processed without the use of
elemental chlorine.

Manning Publications Co.
20 Baldwin Road
PO Box 761
Shelter Island, NY 11964

Development editor: Helen Stergius
Review editor: Aleksandar Dragosavljević
Technical development editor: Doug Warren
Project manager: Kevin Sullivan
Copyeditor: Sharon Wilkey
Proofreader: Corbin Collins
Technical proofreader: Devang Paliwal
Typesetter and cover designer: Marija Tudor
Illustrator: Chuck Larson

ISBN 9781617294396
Printed in the United States of America
1 2 3 4 5 6 7 8 9 10 – TS – 23 22 21 20 19 18

To my mom, my first editor

And to Norma Lee Williams and Richard Allen Kolker,
who each encouraged me to be creative, think critically,
and walk through the world with compassion